W9-AYF-639

OW TO DRAW
MONSTERS
AND OTHER CREATURES

Cheryl Evans

Designed and illustrated by Graham Round and Kim Blundell

Additional design and illustration by Brian Robertson

Contents

2	About this book	18	Giants, ogres and trolls
3	Getting ideas	20	Goblins, dwarfs and human horrors
4	Monster shapes	22	Mythical creatures
6	Drawing dinosaurs	24	Animal monsters
8	Spooky monsters	26	People or monsters?
10	Space aliens	28	Mechanical monsters
12	Sea monsters	30	Techniques and materials
14	Man-made monsters	32	Index
16	Dragons		

Consultant : Jocelyn Clarke

About this book

Monsters come in all shapes and sizes. They can be quite simple or fairly tricky to draw. This book shows you how to draw lots of different monsters and color them to make them look really dramatic.

Shapes to use.

Monster shapes

There are some ideas for monster shapes to start you drawing on pages 4-5.

Dinosaur

Famous monsters

King Kong

Some of the most famous monsters in the world are here, too. Try drawing the Minotaur (page 23) or King Kong (page 25).

All kinds of monsters

There are all kinds of monsters. For example, there are dinosaurs on pages 6-7, space aliens on pages 10-11, and giants on pages 18-19.

Fuzzy alien

Vac-dragon

Unusual monsters

You can turn anything into a monster. Try a vacuum cleaner (page 14), a blob (page 11) or a computer (page 29).

Scary settings

Scenery can make your monsters more exciting. See how to do a watery background for sea monsters on page 13, or a spooky graveyard on page 9, for instance.

Things to use

In this book, you will see how to use pencils, felt tip pens, crayons, chalk and lots of other materials. There is a chart at the back to remind you of all the different things you can do.

Getting ideas

Some of the best monsters come from your own imagination. On this page there are pictures of the kinds of things that can inspire you. You will find ways to use ideas like these later in the book.

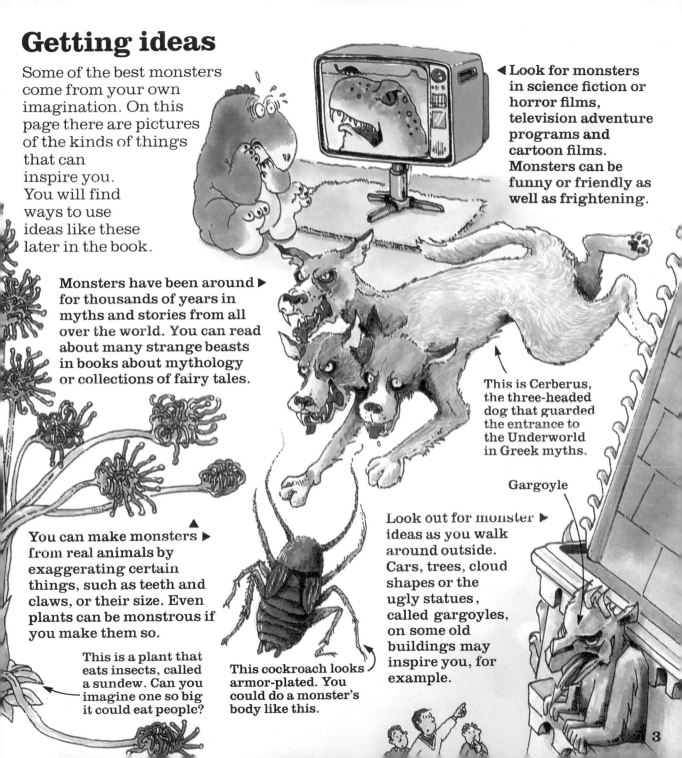

◄ Look for monsters in **science fiction** or **horror films, television adventure programs and cartoon films.** Monsters can be funny or friendly as well as frightening.

Monsters have been around ▶ for thousands of years in myths and stories from all over the world. You can read about many strange beasts in books about mythology or collections of fairy tales.

This is Cerberus, the three-headed dog that guarded the entrance to the Underworld in Greek myths.

Gargoyle

You can make monsters ▶ from real animals by exaggerating certain things, such as teeth and claws, or their size. Even plants can be monstrous if you make them so.

Look out for monster ▶ ideas as you walk around outside. Cars, trees, cloud shapes or the ugly statues, called gargoyles, on some old buildings may inspire you, for example.

This is a plant that eats insects, called a sundew. Can you imagine one so big it could eat people?

This cockroach looks armor-plated. You could do a monster's body like this.

3

Monster shapes

Here are some ideas for monster shapes. Find out below how the shape of a monster can make it look frightening or friendly or make your skin crawl.

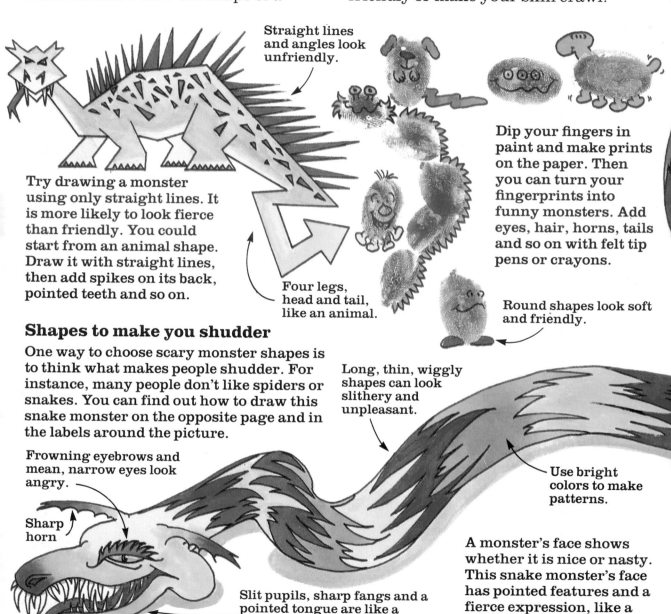

Straight lines and angles look unfriendly.

Try drawing a monster using only straight lines. It is more likely to look fierce than friendly. You could start from an animal shape. Draw it with straight lines, then add spikes on its back, pointed teeth and so on.

Four legs, head and tail, like an animal.

Dip your fingers in paint and make prints on the paper. Then you can turn your fingerprints into funny monsters. Add eyes, hair, horns, tails and so on with felt tip pens or crayons.

Round shapes look soft and friendly.

Shapes to make you shudder

One way to choose scary monster shapes is to think what makes people shudder. For instance, many people don't like spiders or snakes. You can find out how to draw this snake monster on the opposite page and in the labels around the picture.

Long, thin, wiggly shapes can look slithery and unpleasant.

Use bright colors to make patterns.

Frowning eyebrows and mean, narrow eyes look angry.

Sharp horn

Slit pupils, sharp fangs and a pointed tongue are like a fierce wild animal's.

A monster's face shows whether it is nice or nasty. This snake monster's face has pointed features and a fierce expression, like a dangerous wild animal's.

4

Draw a snake monster

Draw a wiggly line. Follow it with another line close to it. Add a pointed tail at one end and a fierce head at the other. Color it in.

Pointed tail ⟶

A friendly monster

Mop of hair looks soft.

Big, round eyes like a baby.

Blunt teeth are not as scary as sharp ones.

Upward-curving mouth makes a smile.

Rounded shapes are friendlier than sharp, spiky ones. This monster's cuddly body, big, round eyes and smiling mouth make it look cheerful and lovable.

Mixed monsters

If you mix shapes it can be hard to tell if the monster is nice or nasty. You could draw some mixed monster shapes of your own, like these. Try to decide if they are nice or not.

Round body, but sharp teeth and claws.

Sharp shapes for body, but smiling face.

5

Drawing dinosaurs

Dinosaurs were huge, real-life monsters that existed on Earth 150-200 million years ago. Here you can find out how to draw and color some of them. You can adapt these basic shapes to make many others.

Tyrannosaurus rex

Tyrannosaurus rex was the king of the meat-eating dinosaurs. It could grow to nearly 15 meters (49 feet) long. The picture in the box below shows you how to draw it. Hints for coloring and other details are shown on the right.

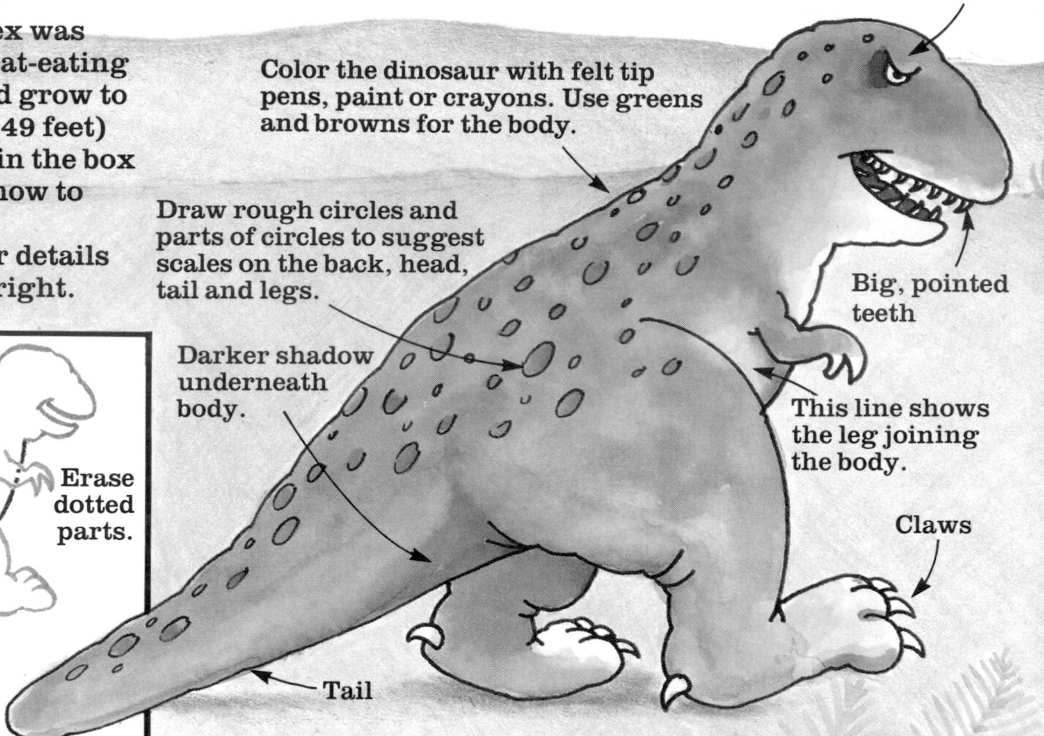

Color the dinosaur with felt tip pens, paint or crayons. Use greens and browns for the body.

Draw rough circles and parts of circles to suggest scales on the back, head, tail and legs.

Darker shadow underneath body.

Eye

Big, pointed teeth

This line shows the leg joining the body.

Claws

Tail

Drawing the shape

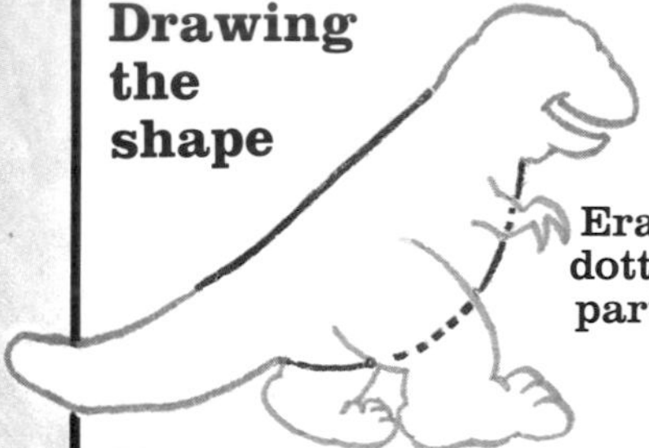

Erase dotted parts.

Use a pencil to copy the lines shown in the picture in this order:

—— First, the black lines.
—— Next, the orange lines.
—— Then the blue lines.

The boxes on page 7 show you how to draw two more dinosaurs. Copy the lines in the same order — black, then orange, then blue.

Giant fern

During the dinosaur period the Earth was warm and covered in dense forests. Plants were giant-sized, though many of them were like forest plants today.

Try drawing giant ferns, like this one, as a setting for your dinosaurs. Do curved lines for stems. Add narrow leaves on each side. The leaves get shorter towards the tip of each stem.

Flying monsters

At the same time as the dinosaurs, there were also flying reptiles, like this pterodactyl. Copy the lines in the box below to draw it.

Scaly body like tyrannosaurus rex. Use brown paint or felt tip pen.

Use crayons for the wings (see below). This contrasts well with the body.

Sharp teeth

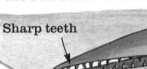

Add wings last.

Wing texture

The pterodactyl has bat-like wings. Get this effect by putting a leaf face-down under the paper and rubbing over it with a brown crayon.

Use a leaf with veins that stick out. A horse-chestnut or maple is good.

Diplodocus

This is a diplodocus. See ► how to draw it in the box below.

You can use the diplodocus shape, or any of the shapes on this page, as a base for drawing other monsters.

Use greys for the diplodocus.

Add an eye and a mouth.

Put a black shadow underneath the body.

Go over darker parts twice.

Diplodocus skin

To get a wrinkly skin texture as in this picture, put a sheet of rough sandpaper under your drawing and color over the top with crayons. Press quite hard. Wax crayons look brighter than colored pencils.

7

Spooky monsters

Ghosts are scary because nobody knows exactly what they are or if they even exist. Some people say they are shadowy, almost see-through shapes that appear in the dark. Here are some different kinds for you to try.

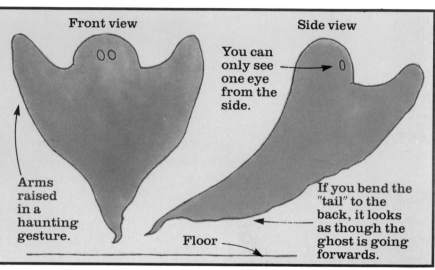

Floating ghost

This floating ghost shape looks a bit like someone with a sheet over their head and arms raised.

Give it a rounded head and wiggly "tail" where its feet would be so it looks as though it is fading away.

Draw the floor below the "tail" so the ghost seems to float.

Front view

Side view

Arms raised in a haunting gesture.

You can only see one eye from the side.

If you bend the "tail" to the back, it looks as though the ghost is going forwards.

Floor

Changing the shape

You can change the shape of a ghost to make it do different things. Give it an expression, too. Try some of the ideas below.

◀ Make a ghost do something normal, like sitting and reading. You can see the chair through the ghost.

◀ Give a furious ghost hands on its hips and an angry face. Do frowning eyebrows and a straight line for a mouth. Red is a good angry color.

Ghostly colors

Here's one good way to do ghostly colors: draw the outline in felt tip pen. Then smudge the line with a wet paintbrush and spread the color inside the shape.

Expressions to try

Why not try some ghostly expressions? Here are some tips to help you.

Friendly: round eyes, curved eyebrows, and a smile. ▶

Surprised: open mouth, round eyes, raised eyebrows. ▶

Sad: eyebrows and eyes slope, mouth curves down. ▶

8

Graveyard phantom

Follow these stages to draw this spooky phantom in an eerie graveyard. It is easier to do than it may look.

1. Make a charcoal patch on white paper with a charcoal pencil or stick.

2. With an eraser, erase a ghost shape, gravestones and blades of grass.

3. Add details with charcoal as in the picture.

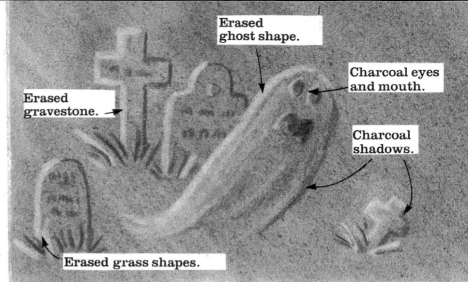

Erased ghost shape.

Charcoal eyes and mouth.

Erased gravestone.

Charcoal shadows.

Erased grass shapes.

Headless specter

Here is another type of ghost. It is in historical costume and has its head under its arm. To draw one like it, use white chalk on black paper. The instructions below should help.

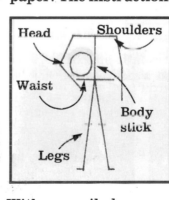

Head

Shoulders

Waist

Body stick

Legs

With a pencil, draw a stick man like this on your paper. Do legs twice as long as the body. Draw the head half as long as the body and to one side. Add lines for waist, shoulders and arms.

Join shoulders and waist. Do neck ruff, bloomers and feet. Add details from the picture on the left. Erase extra lines. Go over the outline in chalk, then smudge it gently with a finger.*

Stop further smudging with fixative spray (see page 30).

Sea monsters

These monsters are all based on things that live in the sea. Find out how to draw them, color them and do a watery background below.

Giant octopus

This giant octopus is splashing in a cloud of its own dark ink so you cannot see how big it is or where all its tentacles are. Perhaps one of them is reaching out to grab you?

You can see half a head and one evil red eye.

Tentacles twist and curl.

suckers.

Add white stripes if you like.

How to draw it

1. Draw the whole octopus lightly in pencil. It has a blobby head and eight coiling tentacles.

2. Mix black and blue paint and, with a brush, splash it on and around the monster, hiding parts of it.

3. When the splashes dry, paint the bits of octopus you can still see black. Add details as shown above.

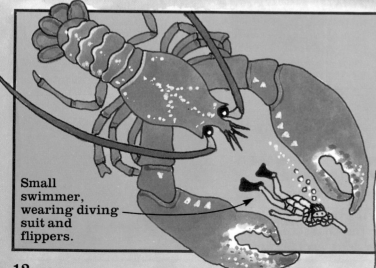

Small swimmer, wearing diving suit and flippers.

Supersized sea creatures

Everyone knows that lobsters are smaller than people. But see what happens if you draw them the other way round, as here.

There are some more small sea creature shapes below. Try doing similar pictures using them.

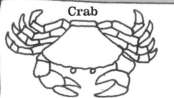

Crab

Sea anemone

Fantastic fish

Invent a fantastic fish monster by drawing a big fish shape like this, with a huge mouth, sharp teeth, bulbous eyes and so on. Find out how to give it a slimy fish skin below.

Staring eyes

Sharp teeth

Spiky fins and tail.

Sharp shapes are scary.

Slimy fish skin

To do a slimy fish skin, first paint your fish with water or very watery color. While it is still very wet, dab on blobs of bright paint. The blobs will smudge and blot to give mottled markings. Paint eyes and other details when the fish is dry.

Water wash

To do a water wash background as on this page, paint clean water all over your paper with a thick paintbrush. While it is still very wet, add watery blue and green paint in streaks. Let them mix and merge. Tape all four edges of the paper on to a flat surface while it dries to stop it wrinkling.

Sea serpent

This sea serpent in the seaweed is colored with wax crayons. If you use them to do an underwater scene, you can put a water wash (see right) on top afterwards because water and wax don't mix.

Drawing the serpent

Draw a wiggly serpent in pencil.* With wax crayon, add fronds of weed. Make some go over the serpent's body and some go behind it. Color the serpent with wax crayons, except where the weeds go over its body.

*See how to draw a snake shape on page 5.

Man-made monsters

If you can imagine things like a machine coming alive or a bad-tempered house, you can make monsters out of almost anything. Making something that is not alive look as if it can think or move is called anthropomorphism. See how to do it here.

Household horrors

Imagine household objects coming alive and doing things of their own accord. They may be nice, but you can make them horrible, like this stove and vacuum cleaner.

Crazy stove

In the box on the right is an ordinary stove shape. On the far side of it you can see one that has been made into a stove monster.

Vac-dragon

This vacuum cleaner turns into a dragon with a snaky neck. The sucking part becomes a head with a wide mouth. Just add two evil eyes and feet with claws.

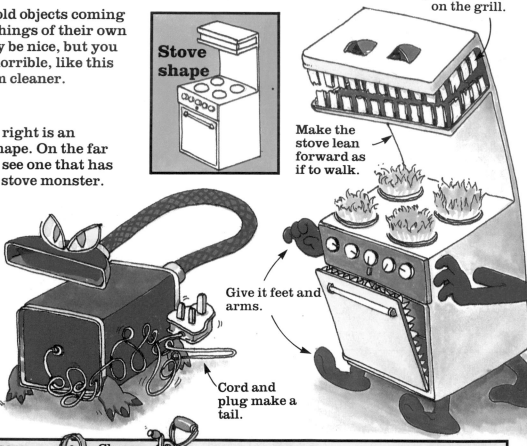

Stove shape

Put eyes and teeth on the grill.

Make the stove lean forward as if to walk.

Give it feet and arms.

Cord and plug make a tail.

Kitchen shapes

Scissors

Cheese grater

Egg beater

Here are some kitchen shapes to turn into monsters. Copy them and add eyes, arms, legs and teeth as you like.

Mean streets

On a dark night, in a badly lit street, a row of houses can look menacing.* Windows turn into eyes and doors look like mouths. On the left is a particularly horrid row. The shapes are quite simple so you could try drawing your own.

Dark doors look like open mouths.

Bottles on step look like teeth.

Reflections in windows make eyes.

Shadow spider plant

Shadows can easily become monsters. See how the plant below casts a horrible spidery shadow.*

Try it yourself. Put a plant on a table by a wall in a dark room. Shine a flashlight or lamp on it to make a shadow on the wall. Different plants will make different shapes.

To draw it, first do the plant and pot and color them. Behind, put a patch of yellow and then smudge charcoal around the edges. Add the big black shadow.

Add eyes to make a monster.

Smudgy grey charcoal.

Convertible car

Here are four steps to help you convert an ordinary car into a monstrous-looking beast.

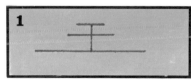

Draw one line down with three lines across it (at top, bottom and a third of the way down). Each line across is twice as long as the line above and is cut in half by the down line.

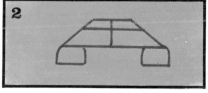

Join the ends of the lines. Do two squares for the headlights below the bottom line.

4 Adapt the shape to make your car look alive. Use curved lines. Make the lights into eyes with slit pupils. Turn the grill into fangs.

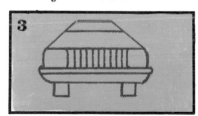

For a bumper do three lines right across below the lights. The wheels are squares below the bumper. Do lines for the grill between the lights.

*See page 27 for more eerie effects with light.

15

Dragons

Dragons are legendary monsters that lurk in dungeons and caves. They can be friendly but many are dangerous. Here are some dragons to draw.

Fairytale dragon

Most dragons have scaly skin, wings and evil teeth and claws. Follow boxes 1 to 4 to draw a dragon. You can see how to color it at the bottom of the page.*

1 Head and neck

Copy the picture on the left to draw the head, neck and bulging eye. Then add nostrils, the other eye and spines down the neck as shown.

2 Body and legs

Draw lines for the top and bottom of the body. Add the legs. Erase the bits shown dotted above.

3 Wing

Draw a fan shaped wing, like in the picture. It looks like part of an umbrella, with spokes going from the bottom up to the point at the top.

Eye sockets

Nostrils

Put darker fingerprints for scales on top of the body color.

See how to color the tail to show how it coils.

Add fiery breath, if you like.

Claws

4 Tail

Add the tail to the back of the body. Join line A to the top of the body and line B (shown in red on the left) to the underneath. Erase the dotted part.

Painting ideas

Body: green
Scales: when the body is dry add darker fingerprints.
Teeth and claws: yellow.

Wings: pale yellow-green. Do the outline and spokes in dark green.
Mouth and eye: red
Nostril: black

*Or use one of the ideas for coloring dinosaurs on pages 6-7.

A dragon's lair

To make a dragon that shines in a dark lair like this one, use colored chalks on black paper.

First draw the dragon's body. Add wings, claws, eyes and so on in contrasting colors.

For the fiery breath, draw wavy chalk lines and smudge them with a finger.

Do rocky walls in yellow. Smudge red and yellow on them to show how they are lit by the flames.

Make heaps of treasure with splodges of orange, red, green and blue.

Glowing dragon

Here is a way to make dragons that seem to glow in the dark. You need wax crayons, white paper and something pointed, like a knitting needle. Follow these steps.

1. Color patches of bright wax crayon. Cover them with a thick layer of black crayon, as above.

2. Scratch a dragon's head into the black wax with a knitting needle*. Bright colors will glow through.

3. Your monster will shine in the blackness, like this.

*Be very careful with pointed things.

Giants, ogres and trolls

There are giants in stories from around the world. They are scary because they are so huge. Try some of the tricks shown here to help you draw them.

How to draw a giant

A whole giant is about seven times the length of his head. The circles next to this giant are the size of his head, so you can see how many head lengths different parts of his body are.

Arms reach about half way down the thighs.

1 head	◯
Neck-waist 2 heads	◯
	◯
Waist-knee 2 heads	◯
	◯
Knee-foot 2 heads	◯
	◯

You can draw people in the same way. They are seven times their head length, too. Children only measure about five of their head lengths, though.

How to make a giant look big

To show how big a giant is, put things in the picture to compare him with. In the picture below, compare the giant to the man, his dog and the trees.

The giant has to bend down to peer at the man and his dog.

A fairytale giant often wears clothes like tied leggings, a tunic and a big leather belt.

Spying giant

Draw a giant spying into a house through the window. You can tell how big he is because his face takes up nearly the whole window frame.

When ogres look small

Castle is far away so it is drawn small.

The ogre is nearly as tall as the tree next to him.

The boy only comes a little way up the tree by him.

The bird is drawn big as it is nearest you.

In this picture the boy is drawn as big as the ogre because he is nearer to you. Near things look bigger than things far away.

In the same way, the trees nearer to you are drawn bigger than those in the distance.

Compare each figure to the tree next to it to judge its true size.

The way things seem to get smaller in the distance is called perspective. You can use it to make pictures look realistic.

Looking up at a troll

If you were standing at the feet of an enormous troll, looking up, he would look a bit like this.

Ask a grown up if you can lie on the floor and look up at them to see for yourself. Their feet look huge, while the rest of their body and head seem small.

The way the parts furthest from you look squashed up and the nearest parts seem to spread out wide is called foreshortening.

See the hints around the picture for how to draw a troll from down below.

Make the legs and body smaller as they go up.

Do a small head with squashed up features.

His hands look big because they are nearer to you.

Draw enormous feet nearest you.

19

Goblins, dwarfs and human horrors

All the creatures on these two pages have a head, two arms and two legs, like people. But these are supernatural beings that live underground, fly at night, or haunt dark dungeons.

Skeleton

This is a spooky human skeleton. It has been drawn simpler than a real skeleton, which has hundreds of bones and is very hard to draw. Follow the instructions round the picture to help you draw one yourself.

Dwarfs

Dwarfs have short bodies and legs, but big heads, hands and feet. They are usually tubby, with bushy beards.

The dwarfs in this picture are in their forge. They are quite tricky to draw. You could trace them, then try to color them yourself.*

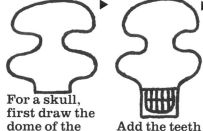

For a skull, first draw the dome of the head and eye sockets.

Add the teeth and jaw.

Color the eye sockets black and add a hole for the nose. ▶

The spine is lots of small bones. Draw them close but not touching.

Ribs curve and get shorter near the waist.

This is the pelvis bone. It joins the spine and legs.

Legs and arms have two long, narrow bones each. See how they join at the elbows and knees.

Use pale grey and yellow to color the skeleton.

Feet and hands have lots of small bones.

Hammer

Faces and fronts lit by flames.

Colors get darker away from the fire.

Tongs

Bellows

Anvil

*See how to mix colors on page 30.

Witch's silhouette

To get the witch's shape, follow these steps.

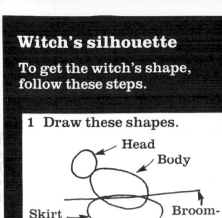

1 Draw these shapes.

Head
Body
Skirt
Broomstick

2 Add details and erase extra lines.

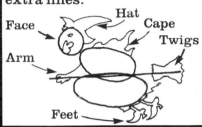

Face
Hat
Cape
Twigs
Arm
Feet

Paint the witch black.

Draw a circle round her for the moon.

Paint outside the circle black for the night sky.

Tunnel disappears into darkness here.

Draw shoulders jutting from the side of its head so it looks as if its head is sunk low.

Do arms reaching below knees.

Drawing goblins

To draw a goblin, do a thin human shape. Give it knobbly knees and elbows and long, skinny arms. Make its head narrow with pointed ears. Color it green with glowing eyes.

Try drawing this advancing horde of goblins in a tunnel. Put big goblins at the front of your picture and smaller ones behind. Make the tunnel floor get narrower in the distance and the walls get closer in. This is using perspective (see page 19 for more about this).

21

Mythical creatures

Myths from all over the world are full of strange creatures. You may already know some of the ones shown here. Try drawing them using the techniques described.

Mermaid

Mermaids are half woman and half fish. They are lovely, but dangerous. They lure sailors to wreck their ships on rocks.

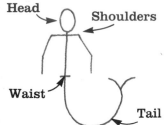

Head
Shoulders
Waist
Tail

To help you draw one, do a pencil guide, like this. Do a straight line to the waist and a curved line below.

Working round the guide, draw a woman's body to the waist and a fish's tail below. Erase unwanted lines.

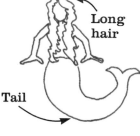

Long hair

Tail

Scales on tail.

Place your mermaid on a rock in the sea and color her like this.

Medusa

Medusa was a Greek monster. She had snakes instead of hair and anyone that looked at her was turned to stone. To draw her, first draw a horrible face. Then add snaky hair. Try printing snakes with string like this:

1. Cut some pieces of string, as long as you want the snakes to be.

2. Dip them in ink or paint and lay them in coils around the face.

3. Put a piece of scrap paper on top and press with your hand.

4. Remove the scrap paper and pick up the string. Repeat to make more prints.

5. Add eyes and forked tongues at the ends of the snaky hair.

Minotaur

The Minotaur was an Ancient Greek monster with a man's body but the head and shoulders of a giant bull. Here's how you can draw him like a Greek vase painting.

Copy or trace this shape in pencil.

Cover the shape, and the rest of the paper, with orange wax crayon. The shape will still show through.

Paint black inside the shape on top of the orange. Use thick poster paint or mix powder paint and glue.*

When it is dry, scrape markings in the black with a knitting needle.

Many Ancient Greek vases are orange decorated with black figures.

Pegasus

Pegasus was the legendary flying horse in Greek myths. Use quite a soft pencil to draw him (find out about types of pencil on page 30). The tips below should help.

Do the outline first. Don't try to do it all at once. Draw a bit then look at the picture again.

Compare parts. Are his legs as long as his wings? How long is his neck compared to his body, and so on?

Shade with light pencil strokes.

Draw curved lines for feathers.

Do lots of strokes for the mane.

Shade the muscle in his neck.

Under parts are in shadow.

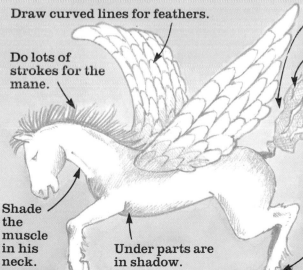

Go over darker shadows twice.

Back and tail are shaded by the wings.

Unicorn　← Horn

You could draw a unicorn. It is like a horse with a single horn.

You can only partly see legs on the far side.

Or you can use black wax crayon, as on page 17.　　23

Animal monsters

People have always made monsters out of animals, like the Minotaur on the previous page. Here are some more, and a game to help you make your own.

Tail

Make ripples by coloring with corrugated cardboard under your paper.

Do as many humps as you like. Make them smaller as they go away from you.

Loch Ness monster

Legend says that a monster lives in Loch Ness in Scotland. This is what it is traditionally supposed to look like.

Chimera

The mythical Greek Chimera had a lion's head, a goat's body and a serpent's tail. Try using different drawing materials for the different parts, as explained below.

Use colored pencils for the head. Mix strokes of brown, orange, yellow and black for the mane to make it shaggy.

Chalk is good for the hairy goat's body. Smudge brown chalk all over, then use charcoal for details and shading.

Smudge shadow under legs.

Legs shaggy at the top.

Use felt tip pens on the serpent's tail for contrast. Use two shades of green and put black scales on top.

Do hooves and outline black.

Shapes to draw

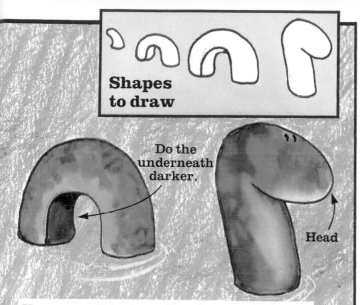

Do the underneath darker.

Head

Use a pencil to draw the shapes of the monster, shown in the box above. Color them greeny-black. For the water, do patches of green and blue wax crayon. Lay the crayons on their sides and rub.

Animal monsters game

Make your own strange animal monsters by playing this game.

Draw a head at the top of a sheet of paper. It can be a real animal's head, or an imaginary one. Fold the paper so only the end of the neck can be seen.

Pass it to a friend, who adds a body. Fold again so just the end of the body is seen.

Pass the paper on. Someone else adds legs. Unfold the paper to see your creation.

King Kong

King Kong is quite modern, but is already legendary. Try drawing this picture starring him.

Draw the skyscrapers. It is as if you are above them so you can see their roofs. They get narrower as they stretch away from you towards the street below.

Draw the giant gorilla emerging from behind the buildings.* He is dark, but paler underneath where he is lit from the street. Make it night to add atmosphere.

Clouds and moon.

Small plane for King Kong to grab.

*See pages 18-19 for some ways to make him look big.

People or monsters?

All the monsters on these two pages are people of a kind - or at least, they might be.

Yeti

Yetis live in the Himalayas. Nobody knows if they are a type of person, ape or monster. Draw this one on blue paper or paint a blue background.

Paint a shaggy Yeti with white paint on a brush. Use as little water as possible so the paint is quite dry and goes on in rough streaks. Add a blizzard whirling round him.

He seems to blend into the snow.

Werewolf

This ordinary man turns into a werewolf on nights with a full moon. Color him with colored pencils. Use light layers of brown, yellow and pink for skin, and shades of brown for hair.

As he changes, it is as if his face is pulled forward: make his nose longer and his chin stick out; give him a thinner, longer mouth; do his ear pointed and higher up; make him sprout hair on chin, cheeks and forehead.

Fully changed, he is like a fierce wolf. Draw a wolf's muzzle. Add sharp teeth and glowing red eyes. His ears are now on top of his head. He is hairy all over.

You can make a blizzard by spraying white paint from a toothbrush, as on page 17.

Frankenstein's monster

Frankenstein stitched together a sort of man and brought him to life artificially. He escaped and terrorized the neighbourhood. This is a portrait of him.

This picture is lit from above. The shadows are black blocks. Copy the shapes in pencil then color them black. Practice drawing faces like this from newspaper pictures. They often look like blocks of light and shadow.

← Lit from above, there are deep shadows in the eye sockets and under the nose, lower lip and chin.

Portrait of a vampire

Vampires rise from the dead and drink human blood. Draw the famous vampire, Count Dracula, like this:

Draw his head and cape and color them with crayons. He has red eyes, fangs and a ghastly green skin. Do eerie black face shadows as shown.

Do a shadow behind Dracula, the same shape, only bigger. Use paint or felt tip pen so it is blacker than he is.

Try copying the two small Dracula figures on the right and add shadows to match.

Eerie light experiment

To see the dramatic shadows that light can cast on your face, try this:

Sit in a dark room in front of a mirror and shine a flashlight from different angles on to your face.

Compare the shadows you see in the mirror with those in the pictures below. They are most dramatic when the light shines from over your head or below your chin. Also note how the shadow of your body is cast on the wall behind you.

Lit from below, the shadows are on the upper lip, cheekbones and forehead.

Mechanical monsters

On these two pages are ways to draw robots and other machine-like monsters.

Destructobot

This destructobot is quite hard to draw. Try using a grid to help, like this:

Draw a grid of squares in pencil, as at the bottom of this page. Do the squares as big as you like.

Look at the squares one at a time. Copy the shapes in each one on to the same square in your grid. Then rub out the grid lines.

The labels round the picture show you some details.

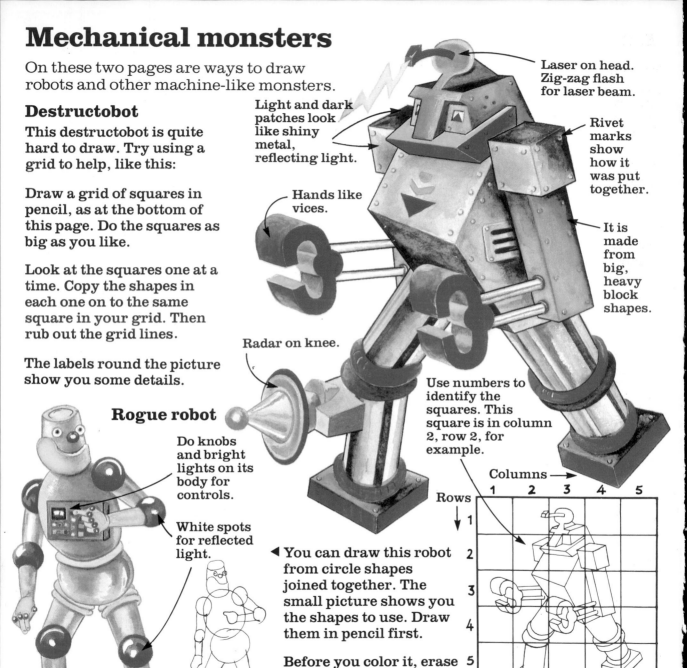

Laser on head. Zig-zag flash for laser beam.

Light and dark patches look like shiny metal, reflecting light.

Rivet marks show how it was put together.

Hands like vices.

It is made from big, heavy block shapes.

Radar on knee.

Use numbers to identify the squares. This square is in column 2, row 2, for example.

Columns ⟶

Rows

Rogue robot

Do knobs and bright lights on its body for controls.

White spots for reflected light.

◄ You can draw this robot from circle shapes joined together. The small picture shows you the shapes to use. Draw them in pencil first.

Before you color it, erase the parts of the lines that are not there in the big picture.

*Put a grid on tracing paper over other monsters in this book to help copy them.

Machine mixer

This monster is made from parts of machines. Try to draw a similar one and shade it with dots and lines.

Use dots on rounded parts. The closer the dots, the darker the shadows.

Use lines on flat bits. Criss-cross lines make darker shadows.

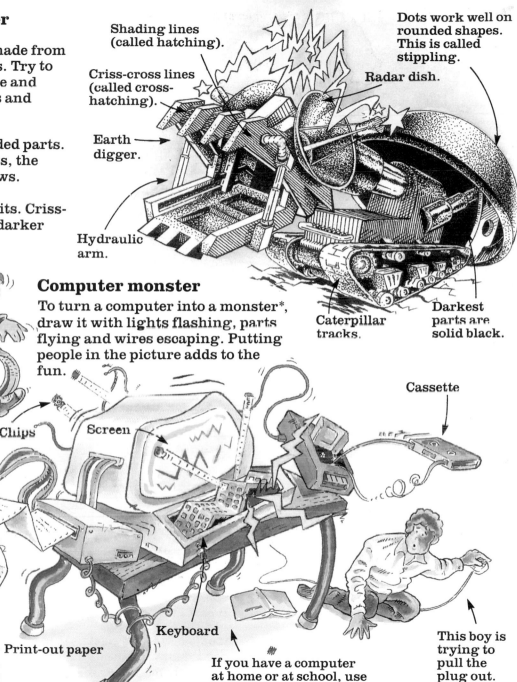

Shading lines (called hatching).

Criss-cross lines (called cross-hatching).

Earth digger.

Hydraulic arm.

Dots work well on rounded shapes. This is called stippling.

Radar dish.

Caterpillar tracks.

Darkest parts are solid black.

Computer monster

To turn a computer into a monster*, draw it with lights flashing, parts flying and wires escaping. Putting people in the picture adds to the fun.

Cassette

Chips

Screen

This cord has swept a boy off his feet.

Print-out paper

Keyboard

If you have a computer at home or at school, use it as a model.

This boy is trying to pull the plug out.

*See more ways to make machines look like monsters on pages 14-15.

Techniques and materials

Here is a round up of all the techniques and materials in this book. The chart on the right has a column for each material telling you how you can use it. A white panel across more than one column refers to all the materials in those columns.

Red

Red and yellow make orange.

Yellow
Blue

Mix red, yellow and blue to make brown.

Blue and red make purple.

Yellow and blue make green.

Mixing colors

This color monster shows you which colors mix to make other colors. You only need red, yellow and blue to make all these colors. (Felt tip pens do not mix like this). Use black to make them darker and white to make them paler.

The pencil family

Pencils can be hard or soft. Soft pencils make thick, fuzzy lines. Hard pencils make thin, clear lines. Most pencils are marked with a code to tell you how hard or soft they are. See how the code works on the right.

2H H HB B 2B

Harder: up to 9 H

Softer: up to 9B.

Most ordinary pencils to write with are HB.

Using fixative sprays

Fixative sprays stop pictures in soft materials like charcoal, chalk and soft pencil smudging. They come in aerosol cans and you can get them from art suppliers. Never breathe the spray or work near a flame. It is best to use them outside, since they smell very strong. Do not throw empty cans on a fire.

Colored Pencils	Pencils
Colored pencils are good for doing hairy effects (see pages 24 and 26).	You probably use pencils the most. You can draw with them first even if you color afterwards.

Drawing lines

Use the point of crayons, pencils or charcoal pencils for fine lines and the side of the point for fuzzy lines and shading.

Shading with lines and dots

You can shade areas with lines and dots. See an example of this on page 29.

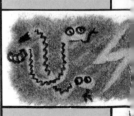

Make different shades with colored pencil by pressing lighter or harder.

Textures

Make textures by rubbing over things placed under your paper (see pages 7 and 24).

Charcoal	Chalk	Wax crayons	Paint	Ink	Felt tip pens

Shading

Lie a stick of charcoal, chalk or a wax crayon on its side and rub. Snap the sticks to make them smaller if you need to.

Spots and splashes

Paint and ink are liquid (paint may be powdery or hard but you add water to use it). Drop blobs of paint from a brush (see page 13), or shake ink blots from a nib. Spray paint or ink from an old toothbrush (see pages 11 and 26).

Thick felt tip pens are good for making solid areas of color. Thin ones are good for lines and details.

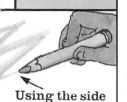

Using the side of the point.

Chalk shows up well on black paper.

Use chalk to help make double prints (page 10).

Scrape shapes into layers of wax crayon (page 17) or into paint on top of wax (page 23).

Hatching
Draw lines like this across the part you want to shade.

Cross-hatching
Draw two sets of lines criss-crossing for darker shadows.

Stippling
Shade with dots. More dots, closer together, make darker areas.

Smudging

Smudge soft pencils, chalk and charcoal with your finger. (See the fuzzy monster on page 11, for example.) Use it for fire, clouds, fur and so on.

Use wax crayons and chalk to make double prints, as on page 10.

Washes

Make a wash background with streaks of paint or ink on paper soaked with water. See how on page 13.

Using an eraser

Use an eraser to make marks in pencils, charcoal and chalk. See an example on page 9.

Wax and water don't mix. You can use this to make good contrasts (see page 13).

Prints

Dip your fingers in paint or ink and make prints. See some ways to use them on pages 4 and 16. Try making prints with other things, such as those shown below.

Felt tip pens come in lots of colors — even luminous ones — but do not mix well. You can use dark ones on top of light ones, though.

Try using coins, feathers, wood. Textures show best with crayons, pencils, charcoal or chalk.

Cotton spool
Matchbox
Polystyrene chip

Index

about this book, 2
animal monsters, 3,4,24-25
anthropomorphism, 14

Cerberus, 3
chart, 30-31
Chimera, 24
colors, mixing, 30
computer monster, 29
convertible car, 15
crazy stove, 14

destructobot, 28
dinosaurs, 6-7
diplodocus, 7
double space scene, 10
Dracula, 27
dragons, 16-17
dragon's lair, 17
dwarfs, 20

eerie light experiment, 27

fairytale dragon, 16
fantastic fish, 13
fingerprints, 4,16
fixative sprays, 30
floating ghost, 8
flying monsters, 7
Frankenstein's monster, 27
friendly, fuzzy alien, 11
friendly monster, 5

gargoyle, 3
getting ideas, 3

ghostly colors, 8
ghosts, 8-9
giant fern, 6
giant octopus, 12
giants, 18-19
glowing dragon, 17
goblins, 21
graveyard phantom, 9

headless specter, 9
household horrors, 14
human horrors, 20-21

King Kong, 25
kitchen shapes, 14

little green Martian, 10
Loch Ness monster, 24

machine mixer, 29
Martian, 10
materials, 2,30-31
mean streets, 15
mechanical monsters,
   28-29
Medusa, 22
mermaid, 22
Minotaur, 23
mixed monsters, 5
monster shapes, 4-5
moon blobs, 11
mythical creatures, 22-23,
   24

ogre, 19

Pegasus, 23
pencil family, 30
people, drawing, 18
   or monsters?, 26-27
perspective, 19,21
pterodactyl, 7

rogue robot, 28

sea monsters, 12-13
sea serpent, 13
shadow spider plant, 15
skeleton, 20
slimy fish skin, 13
snake monster, 4
space aliens, 10-11
spooky monsters, 8-9
spying giant, 18
sundew, 3
supersized sea creatures, 12

techniques, 30-31
troll, 19
tyrannosaurus rex, 6

unicorn, 23

vac-dragon, 14
vampire, 27

water wash, 13
werewolf, 26
witch, 21

Yeti, 26

First published in 1987 by Usborne
Publishing Ltd, 83-85 Saffron Hill,
London EC1N 8RT, England.
© 1987 Usborne Publishing Ltd.

The name Usborne and the device 😀 are Trade Marks of
Usborne Publishing Ltd.